The Lepidopterist

Philippa King

The Lepidopterist
Copyright © 2015 by Philippa King
All rights reserved.
ISBN 978-1517432126

Cover Artwork "Butterfly and Moth Self Portrait"
Copyright © 2013 by Philippa King
All rights reserved.

I have a diagnosis of schizoaffective disorder, bipolar type. This means I experience symptoms of both schizophrenia and bipolar disorder. Writing has been vital to me in my journey of relapse and recovery, through a year-long stay in a psychiatric hospital against my will, through manias, depressions and psychosis, through times of clarity and times of confusion. Butterflies are an enduring theme in my work, both a symbol of the human psyche and a sign of hope.

Philippa King

The Lepidopterist

Philippa King

Lepidopterist - one who studies butterflies and moths.

A Picture's Worth

It buzzes: my mad infatuation with writing
like a beige-grey moth to an incandescent bulb.
And it burns, all jittery, my hunger, my hunger,
far more than I thought: a hot wordy sickness.

What will I not take for it?

You photographed your exhilaration of the midday sun
in the lens for me, encircled by a rainbowish rim,
and the cemetery in the snow some winters ago.

But you should know – I will turn them into a thousand words.

Blue Butterfly

Tell me my sick failings
are not the gravel-stones
you throw at my hospital window.
I believe even the Common Morpho butterfly
in its hazy blue-moon pearlescence
can be found in England
as boxed dead specimens, or living in glasshouses.
I could cause tremors under your thoughts.
For heaven's sake,
don't you think I know what it means
to make a mistake?

The Butterfils

My thoughts, my thoughts
are the batterflies of Fukushima.
I think in flapperbyes like misfolded origami.
My ideas cannot take flight
because although the cappertillers hatch,
none of the flutterkillers recognises themselves
with their own eyes.
So the blufferties grow stunted
and deformed, yet they are still mindful
of what their perfection is to look like.
God will be over the moon at what I know.

Butterflies in the Stomach

It went unspoken before
when I got my mouth burnt
on vodka and lime,
trembling with adrenaline.
The warmth was like your word kept.
I believe butterflies smell with their antennae
and taste with their feet.
Sometimes, my love, our love,
is not enough. It is Sunday. It is January.
I know what year it is.
As the ambulance comes,
I suspect that
I could have been anything and amazing
like skin which seals itself after an open wound.
But I am a butcher,
how am I to help what I was born to be?

Bug Days

Strapped down on a gurney, I know
everyone is a liar: you are not you.
I lie flat like a Blood Vein moth.
Yet did I not dance in the field like a fairy?

'You' sit by my bedside and read to me
the books of my childhood.
I cannot sleep without the light on.

Like finding dawn's exact moment,
it had grown hard to determine
where I ended and where the world began.

Did I not cry? Did I not grin?
I am the caterpillar of what is to come.

The Round

Whose is the white coat,
whose is the black?
The girl over there
tried to cut her own throat.

Here is the doctor,
here is the priest.
This is the ward round,
behind the locked door.

Treatment

Someone has been found guilty
of medicine-dilution,
drinking too much water.
Now the staff have cut the water off
to punish us all.
I am on lithium.
My words die.

Clock

This door is locked.
I should show some restraint:
I can hear me shouting
like crazy in the other room.
My mouth believes
I will get better in here.
But the clock on the wall
has depression
and nothing else to say.

Television

The TV minds us.
I mind the TV.
It speaks my name
and troubles to talk to me
more than the nurses do.

That time they wanted me to try Lithium again

My first word was 'no'.
I knew the weight of it –
as an awkward child –
always a 'no' –
and now as an adult.
My hands flutter around me
like moths disturbed
by a light going out.
No. Still, no.
The word bleeds outwards in the air,
like an ink blot.

The Straitjacket

Is that the question?

I wonder if you know of the North American butterfly,
the 'Question Mark', with its curious taste for carrion –
and will it always bring up thoughts of me?

What if I confess to eating the butter? Yes, I am fatter.
That is evidence against me. You pretend you are my friend, my nurse,
but you tell lies and I only first met you this morning.

Bright Monarchs are poisonous like milkweed, if you please.
Mama, it's me; if I don't go now, they'll call the police.
Buckeye butterflies intimidate by their big wing spots.
In the rainforest, the Blue Morpho lays eggs like rainwater drops.

The glasswinged butterfly,
Greta oto, is see-through.
I've made nothing up.

No-one else but my lawyer knows I am here.

Still Life with Carafe and Oranges

You stand there
like you believe that
I love to live. I lied.

I've gone belly-up,
an image on your retina
before your brain puts it right.

My mind is unbreakable,
a teardrop turned on itself
to form a perfect 'O'.

Now the only word which comes to me is 'no'.

The Butterfly Effect

This butterfly will not dream up
hurricanes again. I promise.

Anxiety prickles my name.
You have watched me snap.
Poisons and pins will be brought.

I don't know where this will go
but I've been here so long,
I now believe even butterflies die.

I remember you

I remember you,
like a warm summer day
in midwinter. You are
the Large White butterfly,
all tattered and beat-up
with those greenish Easter-egg eyes
and fuzzy wings that I saw that time.
I am absorbed by this mention of you,
recalling how a Gatekeeper perched rapt
on a big daisy which smelt of decay.
No-one else comes close to my heart
like no-one else ventured near
those stinking daisies in the heat of summer.

Absent

Someone has walked through the wildflowers.
I have taken many things in order to bring me down.
My pulse has blown my pupils odd and wide,
and the laughter from me is wild, fluttering –
as if the more we hear it, the less I make sense.
I've swallowed a butterfly whole with my eyes
while it danced on yellowing leaves. Ringlets may have eyespots
virtually absent or large and distorted on the undersides.
Did I get that right? Meadow grasses are food
for Gatekeeper caterpillars: fescues and bents. Am I alright?

I'm fine. I am fine. I smile.

I think you should know

my foot has died under me. It is cold
to the shudders
running down the back of my leg,
all the way from my thoughts,
pinched in the hinge.
I might have been there forever
but the family lawyer got me out.
I pretend my foot has not vanished,
so people will still tell me
I'm 'looking well.'

Purple Emperor

– The higher you fly, the further you have to fall.

It's me. But it's mania.
It's mania like a grotesque,
outrageous fancy dress outfit.
My mouth is a Purple Emperor butterfly,
flittering wildly,
full of expletives and obscenities.
Do you know of the Purple Emperor?
In life, it feeds on excrement and death.
You do not know me. I don't know me.
I just want a taste of death
but I can't settle
like those metallic wings
in the treetops.

Elsewhere

I am in pictures of elsewhere.
Someone I do not see
squeezes my hand
and calls my name
at times and often.
So now, I realise
I am really in a hospital
somewhere else
deep in a coma,
and this is all in my head.
It must be that
this is all in my head.

Tangled

It didn't come out quite right.
I've been drinking vanilla vodkas.
I'm unsure of what next –
like an amateur escapologist
in a trick gone desperately wrong,
tangled up on myself,
suspended straitjacket and all.

Large Copper (Extinct)

I memorise blank spots where prescription painkillers have been –
a moth eating holes in cloth. They are mine. I am guilty.
I have lost what I do. I have known the resistance of the flesh too much. A moth too close to the flame is gone.

Under the sun, two white butterflies spiral up
into painful blue until my eyes shut.
The ichneumon fly is a parasite of the larval Large White.
The Large Whites eat the cauliflowers next door down to a stalk.

Large Coppers are gone from here forever.
Someone I do not see calls my name and squeezes my hand often.
What would you say? I look through my eyelids.
A fat caterpillar is eating the seedling cabbages: all our leaves are lace.

Dead Affair

I have been missing.
There is no recollection of the last hour.
I have evidence though –
a pharmaceutical tablet slab
and some spidery handwritten notes.
This evening, I found a small moth
squashed flat between two pages
of a book I picked up,
and I thought of missing you.

Butterfly Watch

Was I 'all there' that afternoon? No.
No. I had seen the Green Hairstreak butterfly,
flitting like a fairy, flitting like I was,
unaware of my own absence.
I'd been drinking again.
I no longer recognised sleep,
at the flashpoint of rage,
and in the fever of fatigue,
my eyes, dry, and gritty as sugar.
My pictures came out blurred, sun-flashed.
At supper, finally, my smile fell.
I watched it suddenly switch
upside down in the stainless steel face of a spoon.
Then, there I was – gone.

Crows over Wheatfield

All at once,
the birds explode into flight.
The air cracks.
We are good people,
we tell ourselves.
Yet war is only ever a stone's throw away.
Why can't I see you anymore?
Someone who is not there
shoves me in the shoulder.
And something's wrong.

Nicholas de Staël

You had left early
but I felt I was lingering
there in that concert hall,
before the grand and the double bass –
the only two
to stay on stage
when all the others have moved off
and the music is silence.

Vincent van Gogh

The wheat whispers to soothe itself.
The field bristles with an anxious laugh.
They say birds take flight
seconds before explosions or earthquakes.
The crows cry, "Why, why, why?"

Sonia Sekula

I hang open
like an animal carved in half,
on a hook,
like a side of meat.
Anyone can look.
Paint turns us inside out.
What am I?
What could overcome that?

Agnes Martin

People like boxes,
neat compartments, orderly.
People put others into boxes.
You cannot keep butterflies
in squares on paper, but perhaps you tried.
You got sick of it
and turned your back.

Sciatica

A nerve is hooked
in the base of my back,
the bones stacked
like dirty coffee cups.
An opioid-like blurs me
to forget
the nervous twinge.

Poppies

I've panicked.

In a split-second,
a legion
is blown out
because God intervenes.

I am the buzz of painlessness,
of synthetic silence,
all fizzy and plastic.

I will not learn this:
my black, vacuous pupil squints,
a lazy eye – always –
to the kamikaze pill.

Someone is going to get hurt.

Amanita virosa

I have not yet heard from you:
it's been eight months.
I said you were an angel,
right from the start
when you wrote,
like chancing upon an abundance of chanterelles
in the forest.
You promised me
the earth, your dark secrets like risky kisses.
But this silence is a hiss.
Everything went white.
And would you know how commonly *Amanita virosa*
is mistaken for the edible meadow mushroom?

The Buzz

We live for the buzz
but it near-kills me.
Like a rabbit in the headlights,
I'm stunned frozen
by sweat prickles and sedatives.
Something hit
a rabbit on the road
going down to town.
It has a crown of flies.
We live for the buzz.

Night may fall, but it is day that breaks

A butterfly may lay a hundred eggs
but only a few ever make it.
I had a hundred ideas.
This heatwave is from the Sahara.
My depression stifles.

The White Butterfly

My face has gone white,
my fingers are white,
my thoughts, my lips –
all gone white,
clamped down in shock.
It bubbles up thoughts
of this handsome frog I saw
uglily gulping down
what is left of a white butterfly,
a hindwing sticks out
of its mouth.
All can do is close my eyes
to my everyday,
to everyone,
to everything
as the whiteness
awkwardly swallows and saps –
what good am I to anyone.

Apathy

For crying out loud,
can't I show some emotion for once?
My mother weeps for me.
I am speechless.
You shake me;
you could shout.
I have no feelings either way.
It's just that I'm caught out in the cold.

The Lepidopterist

Yes, I know the meaning
and the price of freedom.
What I am doing is nothing
short of madness.
This grows to a sickness, an obsession.
You were happy for a moment -
for happiness exists in moments only.
Now all you can hear is me
coughing and spitting.
I have slipped through the net.
You are now no more to me
than the ocean floor to a butterfly.
Yes, I know the meaning
and the price of fear.

Lorazepam

I close down on the blue pill on my tongue.
Do not think I take my life lightly.
Already I am dead-heavy on my bed.
I am fixed –
my green eyes fixed
mindlessly on the wall.

Predators

That white butterfly finally died,
half-eaten and mauled by a wasp,
severed where abdomen and thorax meet.
I did not have the heart to kill it.
It could not fly so I picked it up.
Once I tried to jump from my window –
I believed I could fly.
It trembled in my hand.
I think it knew.
All along, I've known.
I've known that bite.

July

For Julie

My July, my late July
spits the hailstones' hiss,
almost opioid-like, hypnotic,
from a sky of pure blue.
Comma, Comma, fly away, ragged Comma.

It is so cold –
hard as hailstones, and cold -
no wonder all our butterflies have disappeared.

Painted Lady Butterfly

The egg laid by a Painted lady
is the size of a pinhead.
I have put my pen down,
leaving a mark like a dead full stop,
the size of a pinhead.
What could come of things now?
I'm in awe of a big butterfly
wavering over the buddleia.
If only I could move myself
out of the shade.

Aberrations

No-one chooses the way to be born.
What am I – a one-off, an error?
I have been relentless as the midday summer sun,
so full of unsprung energy,
the night has not occurred to me
for a whole four days. The neurotransmitters
are butterflies on mass migration.

Is it today, is it still today?
This is where nothing feels; it does not light up.
Yet, none of us has thoughts of death.
We close our eyes to it.
Here is the colour we have always known, perhaps it is
heaven.

Half a Moth

What could have dreamt
these gold-leaf wings to pieces?
The shadow is bitten in two.
Was it my psychic poisoning through voodoo pins,
or our thought's adrenaline?
Was it jealousy, or silence?
But I'd know how silence kills.
Yet was it an unthinking reflex
which stole the golden breath,
and left September beheaded,
half of itself missing,
on my doorstep this morning?

Butterfly Love

I thought you loved me.
When lit from above,
the male *Lamprolenis nitida* butterfly appears matt brown;
lit from the front, it looks green to red;
lit from behind, it seems blue/violet.
I thought I saw kindness in you.
Meanwhile, he shimmers like a hologram
in the forests of New Guinea.

Dreams

What are dreams made of,
these flickers of the mind's eye?
Neurotransmitters.

Death's Doorway

I caused a ruckus
in death's doorway,
though it was early in my day.
I made a din but death was not in –
so I went away.

Late Last Night

Late last night, I Googled 'death',
like a lab rat gnawing at its cage –
as if he had a Facebook page.

Imposters

Everyone is pretending.
No-one can be trusted.
I deal with duplicates,
forgeries of people,
the same and not the same.
Words don't mean what they say.
They do not taste like that.

The world's askew.
You are an imposter, too,
a replica-copy of you.

Note

Is there nothing I can say?
There is no way –
the heavens close -
and it is dark.
Despair hit the dead-end.
Is there nothing anyone can say?
I'm tired. I tried,
I did. But even this effort
can't go on.

To Asphyxiate

I blacked out
the thought of you,
until my rapid, violent breaths
hurt too much.
Forcing death's door is not easy,
no matter what they say,
even by suffocation
with a plastic bag,
even after a handful of sedatives.
I have tried myself.
Guilt stains, and my God,
I am the traitor who doesn't come clean.

Gynandromorph Butterfly

For the dual-sex Great Mormon butterfly (Papilio memnon) hatched at London's Natural History Museum, 2011, now in the museum's Lepidoptera collection.

I is for imago.
I is for interfusion.
I is interesting and incredible.

My mis-separation is a bilaterally-divided thought,
half-male, half-female,
welded skilfully down the middle.

I am your idée fixe. I am 'it'.
I am around one in ten thousand.
Iam aroundo nein tenth ousand.
I amaro undone intenthous and.

Big Butterflies, Small Butterflies

The Queen Alexandra Birdwing,
with a wingspan of up to a foot across,
is the world's largest butterfly.
It frequents the high-up topmost canopy
of the rainforest of Papua New Guinea.
In years to come, it may be extinct
for we are clearing its habitat from the Earth.
But we may marvel at specimens
in our museum collections,
like the pair caught in Edwardian times,
in a naturalist's crosshairs,
and peppered with buckshot,
the only way to pin such beasts down.
The smallest known species of butterfly
is the Barber's Blue of South Africa.
It is easily missed for its size.
So tell me, my friend, what must I do
to capture your thoughts and,
in all this while, have you missed me?

Dear

For L. because even you don't know who you are.

I don't know if a person
can die of disappointment:
I'm finding that one out.
I woke up again this morning.
Believe me, I didn't mean for you to
trip upon the threads of my undoing.
My bruised knuckle joint,
an army of non-metal helmets,
counts ways to lose – I should not.
You have my faithfulness, my friendship,
my memory, a slipknot.

Love...

It's hard to lose,
and I should know –
part of love is holding close,
the rest is letting go.

Mercy and Love

Your tears are my tears;
my laughter is yours,
and you're laughing now
all just because
the lonely will feel that they're not alone,
and the lost will find that they're coming home.
Mercy and love:
you give and you'll have.
Mercy and love.

Symmetry

A butterfly walks across my fingertips
but my hands are hardened.
You whisper a kind wish for me;
my heart is hardened.
With you, I smiled so much,
and cried so hard.
We are drops in the ocean.
You write on your side, I write on mine.
Perhaps, we left it to drift apart
like the continents from Pangaea.

Yet you wrote again –
and I only now discover your Mourning Cloak butterfly
is the same as our Camberwell Beauty.

Still Life with Red Apple

It cannot sit and read a book.
Yet it shines.
It does not make sense.
But it shines.
Its skin is unafraid to hold my thoughts.
And it shines.
My cheekbone
is an overachievement in bluish bruising.
I was an A* academic all-rounder once.
Now I cannot think how.

Still Life with Hung Rabbit and Copper Kettle

Its muscle
hung
by the hind legs,
once tight sprung,
is now limp, slung
on a loop of rope.
Its fur is not warm,
not like the copper kettle ,
besides,
the fire is gone
from the eyes
by the ring of quick wire,
or the snap, or the shot.

Almost August

It is almost August. I know.

I think you should see
that where life does not kill you,
it only serves to wear you down.
We carry on with the thought
that after this, if we could just get through this,
when this is passed,
things will get better. But what would I know?
I am merely an off-white butterfly,
wings fleckled like vanilla ice cream,
on a large strawberry leaf in a sunspot.

It is almost August. I know.

A Birth Day

You bled me difficultly,
a bubble of stressed syllables
in warm fluid.

My birthdays come at a bad time.
I smile crazily
but my words upset the air,
start wildfires, bubble mushroom clouds.
There is never enough oxygen,
never, never enough.

Poisoned Sleep

The staff
of the science department
at my old school
are poisoning my sleep.
It seems
they have a machine
to beam obscenities
into my brain.

Alone

I want
to be left alone,
I say,
sweating through my jacket.
Now it starts.

Fireworks

We lived in the hospital.
The firework you threw
banged at our window.
The police were called.
They were often called.
I felt for them.
We were paper-thin,
delicate as late butterflies.
To me, that big bang
was a new world being born.

Today

Take today away.
I won't cry or care
when the bedside light is put out.
I might just soften
like a fist relaxed.

I push you away
like I'm pushing everything away.

Mental State

My head hurts like crazy
for the fourth week running.
You worry it could be something fatal.
That feels like a good idea
as if I'd thought of it myself.

The professor asks me
why 'a rolling stone gathers no moss'.
I don't want grass stains.
Then he wants to know
the name of our Prime Minister.
I laugh.
You know that you're in trouble
when they ask you that,
and I can't remember his name.

Suicide Watch

There is an incident.
You claim to be a 'fellow Christian',
saying I'm going to hell
for my wish to die.
I do not speak.
What could *you* tell *me* of hell?
A knife would unnerve me now –
turned on myself -
once you are through feeling,
then it becomes easy - too, too easy.
I am still. I sever myself.
Do not think I trespass here lightly.

Prayer

I praise God
for the gift of my limitations.
Life has brought me to my knees.

Voices

Someone I do not see says
"They should put people who shout,
in a cave,
by themselves."

The notes on my wall
are from God.
They flutter in the breeze
like Monarch butterflies
gathering on the trees
in Mexico.

Now a butterfly
skits so free near
the spider's web.
I've stayed so still.
And I look on.
It had been yellow.

Fancy Dress Party

As a child,
I loved dressing up
with gloves on
both hands and feet.
But now take down the balloons.
Do away with the surprise party.
Today is my thirty-third birthday.
But I've seen this before.
I've had it already.
I blow out the candles on my cake,
wishing to extinguish my air.
Still, here is my smile.
This is my laughter.
How I long for a fancy dress costume
and some face paint –
for I see I am the only one
to have come as myself.

The Light of the World

You think of me,
and I'm right by you.
I want none of this
place anymore.
They say you are the Light of the world,
and I believe you.

Gloria

In a forced Occupational Therapy art class
in the hospital, you laughed at my clay horse
as its last leg fell off, and you wrote across your drawing –
"Gloria in excelsis Deo." Did anyone know what it meant?
I kept silent. I'd been a Latin scholar.
It stood out to me. Out of 19 others in that room,
no-one knew you had uttered an unknowing prayer:
"Glory to God in the highest." So I shouted a sudden 'Amen!',
startling everyone. It was noted down that I had lost it.

The Glasshouse

I look blank.
So is it my fault,
is it my fault again,
that the enclosure doors were left open
and all the butterflies
fluttered out
amongst onlookers?

Index

A
Aberrations, 40
A Birth Day, 58
Absent, 15
Agnes Martin, 27
Almost August, 57
Alone, 60
Amanita virosa, 30
Apathy, 34
A Picture's Worth, 1

B
Big Butterflies, Small Butterflies, 50
Blue Butterfly, 2
Bug Days, 5
Butterflies in the Stomach, 4
Butterfly Love, 42
Butterfly Watch, 22

C
Clock, 8
Crows over Wheatfield, 23

D
Dead Affair, 21
Dear, 51
Death's Doorway, 44
Dreams, 43

E
Elsewhere, 18

F
Fancy Dress Party, 67
Fireworks, 61

G
Gloria, 69
Gynandromorph Butterfly, 49

H
Half a Moth, 41

I
Imposters, 46
I remember you, 14

I think you should know, 16

J
July, 38

L
Large Copper (Extinct), 20
Late Last Night, 45
Lorazepam, 36
Love…, 52

M
Mental State, 63
Mercy and Love, 53

N
Nicholas de Staël, 24
Night may fall, but it is day that breaks, 32
Note, 47

P
Painted Lady Butterfly, 39
Poisoned Sleep, 59
Poppies, 29
Prayer, 65
Predators, 37
Purple Emperor, 17

S
Sciatica, 28
Sonia Sekula, 26
Still Life with Carafe and Oranges, 12
Still Life with Rabbit and Copper Kettle, 56
Still Life with Red Apple, 55
Symmetry, 54

T
Tangled, 19
Television, 9
That time they wanted me to try Lithium again, 10
The Butterfils, 3
The Butterfly Effect, 13

The Buzz, 31
The Glasshouse, 70
The Lepidopterist, 35
The Light of the World, 68
The Round, 6
The Straitjacket, 11
The White Butterfly, 33
To Asphyxiate, 48
Today, 62
Treatment, 7

V
Vincent van Gogh, 25
Voices, 66

Printed in Great Britain
by Amazon.co.uk, Ltd.,
Marston Gate.